The Stranger Dissolves

Christina Hutchins

The Stranger Dissolves

POEMS

SIXTEEN RIVERS  PRESS

Published by Sixteen Rivers Press

P.O. Box 640663

San Francisco, California 94164

www.sixteenrivers.org

ISBN: 978-0-9819816-2-8

Library of Congress Control Number: 2011-920080

Cover photograph: John Sluder

Contents

If I want to mix a glass of sugar and water, I must, willy-nilly, wait until the sugar melts. This little fact is big with meaning.

HENRI BERGSON, *Creative Evolution*

If you think you can grasp me, think again;
My story flows in more than one direction . . .

ADRIENNE RICH, "Delta"

The Stranger
Dissolves

SPECTRAL SELVES

❧ Elementary Departures

A river blooms and revises the world.
This rendering precedes and inherits me,
a threshold of atomistic thistles and bees.

Each thistle blooms a thirteen-spiked morning
star, rolled round on the chain of wind.
Each bee's drone minutely stabs the day.

Time is pitted—my bare legs, pierced once,
scar. Ice cubes pop from the tray.
Moved by what preceded us, we will be

inherited whole, pointed in every direction.
A lover's fingers bloom in me. Hunger blooms
in a sub-Saharan belly. Angers bloom.

The first taste of rock salt shatters the deer's
previous body. Sunlight spigots forth.

✤ EXCESS

How many days do I want?
As many as I can turn wisely.
And all the excess,
the unwise, unclear, the mottled:
breath become steam on a winter morning
and coiling silent away,

the last and the first leaves,
brown among pliant green,
       green among shattered brown,
the gray threads above my ears
staining my shook dark hair
with unshinings.

I want the days when sun
rattles the seedpod
and nothing happens
but a shadow
   swallowed by other
shadows.

For there are days when nothing
bursts or breaks or is planted,
     when even wheels
fail to turn,
        and burrs
score our ankles without clinging:

days when nothing moves forward,
when twigs and fallen leaves
blot the moist earth,
and the mingled smells
rising cannot be
untangled from the sunlight.

Trick Riders

There is nothing, nothing, nothing two women
cannot do before noon.

ANONYMOUS

That first afternoon of Vermont sun and blue meadow sky
a frisking of cumulus   winds of August trampling the hilltop
we dreamed of balancing our bodies on the loping air
We lay into ravishing the blades of grass

Here in October along San Francisco Bay   fog hovers
all morning   but so thin   the blue atmosphere   outstretched
boughs   eucalyptus mingling atop the hill   could emerge
could grow visible—   only a matter of seconds

and the right salt breeze   a quick breath and your hands on my back
steadying me—   Our future obscured
but not far away   let's make quick work of articulation
Already we have the language of desire   but between words

we need the rising dust   each leaf and jot of ground
a resolute wind—*glad to meet you*—
These delicate depictions   this acquisition of definite forms
will require our whole courage—

Drop the reins and hoist me up   Set your fine feet
where the muscles move   You and I
can climb the wind   a trick horse
already knifing out the gate—

Like water ripples from a tipped pitcher or a blade
presses butter to its melt   stretch out your arms—
I'm here and I dare you   For this the solitary years
working the living breath—

to mount this cantering moment—   silver splitting
down a hillside   juts and folds revealed—   A flash of sun
and the upshifting vapors are twisting away
as   balancing   we stand at full gallop

The Physicist to His Daughter

I am leaving soon,
slipping to where language
will no longer find me,
my days a passage of blue
shadows smudging the linoleum
with wings.

Already I miss my mind at play:
salt flats splayed with meetings
of an incoming tide. I can't point
to the far field and find my way
to where—only a moment ago—
the wild geese rose.

Sedges, grasses suddenly too tall
tear at my clothes,
my bare hands. I am lost in the slough,
                its voices a rabble
laughing, pointing:
I have no words even for this.

So many silvered blades bending,
    I mill, too,
though I worked the lucid
equations of time, figured
energies of matter and apprehended
the rates of decay.

Know that I do not want to forget
your name. I am your father.
I held your small, untamed hand.

When I have forgotten, remember
who I am: expand the universe.
Tarry in every leaving.   Linger,
like the oboe echo after geese,
like the salt on your lip
after a day at the beach.

My head begins to drop at its own weight.

Before I forget: the days are more
kind than unkind.   Music lasts.
There is nothing like this.

❧ Like a tossed rock landed,
(Liberty Bay, Washington)

two sailboats came about and, leaning
hard, crossed paths. Where the wakes met,
a single point, reckoned from the torn

surface, extended into rings:
casual curves of green and feather gray
echoed the event.

The sailors on their different boats waved
and passed close enough to gaze, wordless,
longer than we do on shore,

one gliding toward a narrow mooring,
the other toward deep channels,
the spent mouth of morning.

This is how the afternoon came,
calmly splitting open. A hundred grays
met and turned away.

One gull's pitched escape
    banking,
            dropped down,

        and the curving cry
                spreading its wake
                met the buoyed clap of a bell.

Such a stone liberates the water's
spectral selves. Disturbed, time
itself portals and will splay—

        radiance,   then shadow.

A WOMAN'S DESPERATE HANDS
(Berkeley, California)

Does every afternoon ripen so irrevocably?
A sun no shade tree can tame
bursts and bursts its skin, and millions
of miles cannot stop the rushing.
A wind off the Bay lifted everything

it could: the bent heads of daisies,
old news along a fence. A girl's skyblue
skirt was rung like a bell, the same
breeze exalted the leaves,
and every hair along my bare arms rose.

Walking home, I missed you,
that quick ache, white glint
of the sidewalk, buff of wind, and,
suddenly, a woman's desperate hands
opened against thick glass.

She was shut up in the backseat
of a police car. Cops standing around,
trying not to see her,
I wanted to stop, say to them,
Release her!   Release her now!

wanted to go to the closed window the way
a salt breeze cannot hold itself
but lives by snapping cloth and seeking skin,
wanted to match my hands to hers
on the other side of the glass, to murmur,

It's all right.   The air will move again.
Whatever craziness is in you   on you
in   from   of   this,
you are all right.   But I couldn't say that,
didn't do it, don't know.

The sun surged between mayten leaves,
and, with the certainty of the air that crowds
and claims, I wanted your fingers interlaced
with mine, juice of the day seeping
relentless warm toward dusk.

The woman's frantic eyes sought me,
a window-framed stranger. Irrevocable
as a late June peach, she pressed her hands
soundlessly against the infrangible glass,
until her life, and mine, clamored through.

THE POET TO HER POEM

Make of my elbows small pebbles rolling
the river bottom, a fierce and pummeling sweep.

If you will, build of my limbs and trunk
the supple breast and weight of the water.

Of my hands, eels, my ears
twin leeches sucking sound,

already these feet are two swift fish
flicking the shadowed pull of current.

Of eyes and mouth, shape glints and echoes,
sunlight and voices under the bridge.

If you can make of me water's muscle,
then perhaps you can float:

lay your head where the shoulder of the river rounds,
where the heft of it bends and pools,

hear a river's shifting joints and taste summer
licked from the lips of a swimmer.

Be sure to tell all the tales—laughter and the drownings—
what I have taken and what I leave behind:

whole lives, wide banks strewn with smooth stones,
the yellow foam of pollen painting the shore.

A GREEN AND

RIVEN UNIVERSE

∗ UPSTREAM
(near Eden, Vermont)

In the month of August I came to love
a river. Looking upstream it was all
threshold, a constant labor, falling

ahead of itself to leave itself
behind. Nerved silvers come leaping,
and lifetimes of silence make way:

a shy child becomes the bannered
woman, striding and laughing aloud,
the tenor, vocalizing in his studio,

enters a concert hall, and you,
late-blooming as the evening air,
ascended my porch stair.

The crowd loves a parade. Skycaps
and symphonies persuade: relentless crossings,
thresholds are myriad.

After a day of rain, such a leafy
vapor lingering, open-mouthed
kisses were everywhere . . .

Dreambeast, love, flashflood
of a summer storm, all night
the river was rising high,

cleansing, haunting, and, mounting
each mislaid step,
shifting the living shores.

✤ During Migration

Then let me be always migrating,
en route to summer feeding grounds, nests,
to winter mates gathered where the streams
still run, where steam melts the ice
and hidden hot springs sustain.

Yes, I arrive, but I go again.
I have appeared and will appear, the habitats
strange, and sometimes I will be lost:
sidewalk of a foreign city slapping uphill holding your hand,
a small inland pond fed by nothing but rain.

❧ RIPPLE-HALVES

We lean over the end of a dock in Wisconsin
looking down   forgetting how reflections
distort   because beauty is in the distortion—
red carried on ripple-halves between blue
sky   your sweater broken and disturbed   lifting
over your head and reaching under the dock
smacking the pilings red   red   red

except you may not even own a red sweater
we have never stood on a dock together
though I do have a poem   your self-portrait
beside a boathouse—   *She came to herself,*
for herself—   and me wanting her wanting you
and of course these fish spinning through our bodies
that are only surfaces after all   until

as we've done and will do again   we turn
to each other warm and grasp with our arms
a pleasure so dense   the hollow crafts—
all our language tossed and landed   even water-
striding images streaming out and under—
can convey only scant pieces   cannot be sufficient
as when we take each other and hold on

❧ Beginning

I could walk away now
as if you never existed.
Bury you in the sun,

your face opening brilliant
to me as it has once
or twice. I could sing away

the conversation beside the river,
add your voice to water's
polyphony around the rocks.

But those damn Tennessee vowels,
how *time flies* while your blue eyes
dare calm. Too, the small gap

of Vermont evening when a river
I thought constant   leapt
as it never has nor will again.

Wild vault! Your hand
pulling me from the deep pool, this
unrepeatable moment, this one.

In a Time of War

Your hands on your guitar   one at the neck
the other at the black hole of an open
mouth—   in a time of war do the songs we make
matter more?   Your fingers worked the strings
until wood sang in its curves and the still air quivered

This evocation occurred in Tennessee while in California
at the edge of a grieving and brutal continent
in the small silences between waves
I was listening   the black hole of me
seizing vibrations warped by gravity

                    Some forces change everything
though free space still hovers under a raindrop
under a turning Pacific wave and still
the immense space abides under the fallen towers
just before the collapse   There are stairwells

lobbies and concert halls   tunnels and ancient caves
There are storm surges   footsteps down
and footsteps up   resonant chords
enjoined of strings and echoes   As Annie Sullivan
spilled *water* into the hollow of a hand

spell into air the necessary gestures—   Amplify
the damp breath of the buried   their last exhalations
sought no retribution—   only love—
                    Life so quickly passes
and moments of suffering are years

✦ WILD NIGHT

Well intentioned in the dark I listen to you
breathe. I do not curl around your turned
shoulder, do not roll myself into your dream
nor catalyze your waking. Today you left
your home of years, *goodbye Tennessee,*
and the slow green river I have smelled
cupped in my hands, transparent in the fall of your hair.
Today you left a husband for the Pacific, crossed
state after state to be here with me, grief
a line your mouth draws, even in the dark.
For this night I hold back.
Never hold back, you said. *Never, never*
hold back. Wild with love, I am
the leopard who dares not even pace.

🌿 O Yes

Fasten me to your equipage   It is all
I want   my only want   everything: air   poem   sun

the barely lit night unfolded over me   your hat
set firm on my head by your hand on the brim

Take me everywhere you go   voice all your words   your whistles
pull me through your dreams   If love is excessive so be it

I want only the vegetable labor: standing hip to hip
sink to cutting board   peppers and onions   two knives flashing

the work of crossing city streets   clearing fields   a plow of two voices
among the horns and wheels

Tack me to what moves: curves of wrist   breast   sole of foot
your untucked shirt   guitar pick   the single silver hair leaping askew

Use my fingers as latches   buckles   rope   hook and sinew
zipper tourniquet nail shoelace rivet thorn

whatever fastens and holds: suture   burr   camber of molding
hugging the doorway   My shins and arms for

seams of your coat   sweet fabric laying narrow folds along your back
take my toenails as pendants   my quick tongue for an earring

Fasten me into your hand—   a blue pen daring your mercies
a grasp measured immeasurable   found equal to your own

❦ CLEAVING

As the towers fold inward
two people grab hands, twist down
the great, intolerable air, enter our dreams
embracing, and we wake—

your fingers round my wrist. Only a slim handful,
these days and nights, already your grip frees
definite cleavings—as if for years
I'd read the wrong books

and loved the wrong person, stinted
this liquid and consummate art. Just beyond
our window, the feet of a hummingbird
are two tiny clasps riding the arched hours.

How can bones so fine hold on
in the willowed dark? I've never met
a strength like yours, except
dark-haired Brianna at six—

The tumor at the base of her skull
is gone almost three years now,
and yesterday someone asked, "Brianna,
where is the safest place when you are scared?"

                    Maura and Patty—
Her mothers. "Do you tell them
you are afraid?"   *No—*
          I attach to their leg.

Into the grasp of our first night she'd spoken. "This is
only a time and a place." A *rift.* "Don't wait for me."
What else could I do? Meanwhile I took up
the possible, and, like a searchlight, into its beam
hidden and shifting shapes appeared. Animate and strange
and mine, the banished forms crept forward.
How long had I avoided this lit circle rimmed by the dark?
Years of invisible questions crystallized into breaths
I could see. Delicate breaths, near answer.

Beyond this small light a universe pulses, night sky
of infinite and expanding interstices no lifetime is wide
or wild enough to fully explore. But the desire
is here, is enough. I want my free hand reaching
into the unknown crevice overhead. Want
with the strength of my muscled body to pull myself
into the tear. This is no passive waiting, love.
I am climbing a green and riven universe by this lamp,
unexpected, fitted to my hand.

❦ The Tethered Lip

The love that matters us is a universe
concentrated between our lives

One Sunday afternoon you said
leave it there   my upper lip between

your lips   So I did and woke hours later
my lip still grasped by your mouth—

How was I shifted?   I would learn
the tongue's most tender dark

HAIL

✦ ✦ ✦ ✦ ✦ ✦ ✦ ✦ ✦

❧ HAIL

Six small stones tumbled from the sky
and rested amid the bouncing.

I picked up marbles of ice, wanting to stow them,
to show them off: the dust knows better.

The poet's feet decided to take her to the laboratory.
On the stairs her knees ground the angles of question marks.

Bergson said, *Wait. Wait until the sugar dissolves.*
Is this where my father lives?

Inside the melting I looked down
the vortex of his eyes and saw the greatest human sadness:

the porch door I couldn't open, though there was a day,
waves, such a blue lake, the air's restless fingers.

What does it mean to lose the world by increments?

It is rendered in the stitch by stitch diction of a ripping seam.
In empty pockets of dust along the road, where melting

stones have cratered earth like its moon. Last night
I almost cut off my arms, trying

to usurp my hands. Today my rescued palm's
a cradle where the beautiful stranger dissolves.

A scar tells a little white lie: healing is not a return.
Wait.   The titration is going to pink: let it go.

⚜ Washing My Father's Hands

He situates them directly in the beam of falling
water under the kitchen spigot and waits.
I take up soap and one by one his right
then his left hand in both my own.
We rinse, splashing, and I turn off the faucet,
grasp two proffered wrists, both
at once in an embrace of my toweled hands,   .
and gently pull. I dry his hands
exactly as he once dried mine:
I press my thumbs into his relaxed
palms. Between us terry cloth
becomes the rough-soft world entire,
and from shadows and air, a cloth worn thin,
I gather one by one each yielding digit.

❧ YOUR HANDS, STAINED

with the work of turning earth, you are thirty-nine,
and I am nine years old, my hair long and escaping
barrettes and ponytail, wildly, finely. Your beard and hair,
dark, your glasses black-framed and very thick,
we stand there. Your arms encircle me.

Behind us waits the twig of an apricot tree, too thin
to cast a shadow, and the bare yard waits for us, too,
waits for the lush days of mulberry, lemon, and birch,
of arbor grapes climbing, ping-pong games clipping
the silence, birds' nests, water lifting, collecting,

and planting the light. Purple agapanthus, tomatoes,
corn, peas, apricots split open in the sun,
and those ladybug beetles that one spring chose to settle
into a massive five-day congregation of feasting and flight.
I feel your snug arms around me, loose and freeing,

leaving space for me to grow beyond your shoulder, beyond,
beyond, flying over the fence with the ease and sadness,
the three-note joy of a redwing blackbird.
I do not remember that particular day, but it echoes
exact anyway, a day I carry as I carry

the rhythm of skipping, as I carry the sobs and the play,
snapping towels and taste of water, ache
of growth and rip of grass, as I carry the arc
of so many balls passing between us, arm to arm,
fingertip to fingertip, through sun, ocean mist, evenings

of days and days, the bright terrain, all those days
packed roundly into the stridings and restings of my long body,
into the very features of my face becoming more and more
whatever hints and guesses hovered there
in the shadowed curve of your well-used life.

❧ PAINTING DEPARTURE

Six times, that same open-ended street,
the sidewalk, circling birds, sometimes she painted

maples curbside, gates, garbage cans,
high windows poppy orange, leaves

cluttered green and crimson as if spring and autumn
arrived at once. *Did I live there?* Does she

now reach over a fence, unlatch the swinging gate,
stoop to pull dead blooms from the dahlias,

walk toward a screen door already opening
as she arrives at the bottom step?

Months, then years. The street faded as if washed.
The woman began to avoid

pigments too bright, just as at piercing sounds
she now fastened ancient hands over her ears

and rocked, *too loud, too loud*—as if
life was grown so close

it loomed, intense, and like a child
she refused what came

strong and unbidden. Since infancy she had lived
shielded, scales on her eyes,

veils wrapped round her ears, and now barriers
fell and fell.   The street,

its trees, its houses and old reflected sun
faded, hues approaching the pale

halo of morning on the stuccoed hills, the bleached
sea.   Even her brushstrokes

lightened, as she unweighted her hand,
receding from its imprint.

Until the street was never there.
Maybe the dissolving

is what matters.   Maybe what we hunger for
is the dun grain of a plain bread

torn and left for pigeons or gulls.
The birds circle, quietly land, then lift

away the shattered soft pieces, as if
our hands had never touched them.

and in the silence a poem
I still needed the I
but the I was soaring away
a small lilt of unchecked
sorrow   I tried to shortcut

down the slope between
two roads   Steep   untrod
except by mice   by snakes
by beetles and ants   there on
a small plateau of deer path

was a dead songbird gone
charcoal black   its eye
a hole   its beak open
its black wing half-folded
and going transparent

Shrunken toward earth
the eyeless thing both
decaying and preserved
was trammeled by the delicate
mesh of late summer

stems   In the bird
hollowed out and flattened
was a silence and in that silence
the song-rapt days
kept alive by a heart

going to dust   To release
what is human   the making
takes up socket and ravished
wing and audibly beats
their irrevocable dispersal

To deny the poem would
kill the bird twice—
to kill the bird again
would kill the I who departs
as if from within—

❧ Is it

(for those living and dying with Alzheimer disease)

like the gentle crisis that happens each night, turning
a corner and leaving everything behind? Every night
if we're lucky, at full stride we round

that corner, plunge from ceaseless sun into deep
shade, fall into step with long blue shadows and ease
along a diagonal stripe of light, the avenue

of truths listing strange. A cool breeze loosens
everything: coats, hair. Or, just as suddenly, the pitched
green awnings   still. Maybe it's the easy

pivot on the ball of one foot, rounding a granite
corner and finding yourself midday on a completely different
street. Is it a constant falling

asleep? Or is it a continual crisis, emerging to an unfamiliar
place, stunned with morning? Jarred awake, the steps
taken a moment before already fallen

to fragments. Soft and close along the body, sheets
worn thin cling awhile, milled wrappings of the relentless
dream. A passing shoulder

glances hard. Shoved from a brass standpipe,
the burnish of light leaps, and every face is a stranger.
Warm air rushes from a sidewalk grate,

the vent of an underground train. Pushed ahead
of the train then pulled behind it,
such a tired, bright silver wind.

THE RED BOAT
(Poulsbo, Washington)

You can only find red things by adventuring amid
physical experiences in this actual world.

ALFRED NORTH WHITEHEAD

Venturing alone to town
I smelled blackberries
sweet parabolic risings
all down the hill

The sky married Liberty Bay
and the expanse lapped my hands
so I walked as if I were paddling
the long kayak at dusk

water so still it became trees
and yellow faces   clapboard
houses leaning forward
to touch my boat   My paddle

dipped   swung with small
sounds of tasting: smeared green leaves
the ochre trunks of madrona reaching
When tethered to vast blue   its thin

mast empty   the hull of a small sailboat twinned
and fell toward me unrolling a royal path
            my paddle took it up
dripped tiny red lamps

On the way home   uphill
I wandered among bushes and into thorns
Afternoon fell   parceled
         warm into these cupped hands

I stood and ate until my fingers dripped
blackberry blood between
         every tendon   muscle
and bone   until red

         paths of ripened light
                   crisscrossed and dried
on the brown backs of my hands
where the skin grows thin as paper

LIKE SALT ON THE LIP

CROSSING THE BRIDGE

i.
One poet died, in her dying
took her blood child, and
left behind another poet:
husband, the father of the child.

5 o'clock Friday, *tell me*
your day, my reader was brushing her beautiful
hair, and even the summer doorjamb rejoiced
with late sun. *His wife,* she said. *The child.*

Quick, I dodged a pummeling
weight. Then felt for him a managed sorrow
while for the dead poet nearly nothing—*how*
terrible—I cleared my throat.

ii.
Driving the Bay Bridge, late night
thumped between retrofit plates.
Sweetly tired, and you, my reader, driving,
I let language lead me home.

But in the tunnel through Treasure Island
the dead woman's torment, quiet as a cat,
slipped over us, treading
me under. *How terrible*

her suffering must have been. A merciless
kneading. Darling beside me, we, too,
have traveled very low, been palpated, unbearably.
What could have been, how nearly.

iii.
A tendered, rolling thing, I am
death interrupted by moonwane.
We are out of the tunnel: city lights
shatter; they ride the night waves.

Unseen below, steel pilings dare first the broken
surface, then impenetrable ink, then mud,
and finally, in a place none alive has been,
settle beyond the reach of the pile driver.

The ramparts of the world rest on nothing
but the buried gone to bed.
Only silt now, yet how steadily
it must bear us, reader.

❦ AFTER SAPPHO

*Prehension is how an occasion in its immediacy of being
absorbs another occasion which has passed.*
ALFRED NORTH WHITEHEAD

Sweetest hours of a sweet life
quite literally we became one another

Not the old couple finishing each
the other's sentence but beginning here

adrape   Prehending in such proximity!
My skin the immediate past

of your skin   There are so many
places I can never go:

your pain   dreams   or from them
into your days   Incalculable the loss

the one poem ever requiring
the passed be past

How long ago did this heat I field
depart your animal furnace?

Stay / Go

Even in Hades I am with you.
SAPPHO

The aspens: telling so many truths
or one truth so many times?

Two-fingered needles of lodgepole pine littered the forest floor:

Leave me alone / Will you move in with me?

Rain and sleep had rendered us illegible,
but the hailstorm was a cowbird, dropping
foreign eggs in all the nests of the dust.

Bare-armed in our thin summer shirts
she and I headed for the meadow.
A pen released from its cap,
I bent down to pick up hail.

Damp of hail melting among the trampled
grass, like a mosquito she was suddenly in me
and I in her, irrevocably.   (Hydraulic shunts
lift the scales of this prickly pine wonder.)

Stay with me forever / I never want to see you again.

Strange little gem melting in the contact zone,
moisture seeping between finger and palm,
I, too, have lost myself against
the stored heat of a human hand.

I awakened in the imperative in order to say
what couldn't be said.   At high altitude, how strangely
grateful the single root of aspen grove, the dry
forest floor.   Disassembling the cold stones,

the divergent vectors of lodgepole are two tiny spread
arms. *Read* their myriad embraces: wake, manger,
lever of burnt umber.   Pitched pup tent
on a brown highway sign, beak of the laughing

bird, > greater than and less than <
the twin radii of an untraced circle, a rusted hinge.
A compass, the peace sign, the V of Victory!
Two wings angled steep for landing.

We walked home, hand in hand,
sweating a little, to squeeze our teabags.
To discombobulate her,
I set a pine cone on each chair.

❦ Remainders

We lay abed fitted and refitted
and the remainder of the day could not stop washing
its hands   its face   its long and glossy back

in the passing strands of us   Savored
silk   we were mercurial
the sunlit mane of a river in flood

For years you leaned forward with the dusk
then again away   O house of solitude
damp night air

flax wrapped loose round my dark comb

✿ The Gihon River

The branch called Gihon is the second
river that flows out of Eden.

GENESIS 2

Raw juice of another mango burned
While all afternoon others napped and read
I wielded the big knife through unmanageable
softness   the flesh-clung pits—
waited for the moments after supper   for the river
to take me whole in its fragmenting hands

Months later her fingers had entered
where others had been   where I'd yearned
and been satisfied   But when she
touched   I took and around her
fragmented   Her hand was
a voice   vowel and muscled

consonance   longed for since creation
and offered—   glorious the moments
when fear ceases exacting its cruelty
hoarding tiny signifiers into myth
and I lingered years
              unwritten along her skin—

Under the tough blush of every mango
rests the softest striated muscle
but through that hot kitchen afternoon
the juice found each small wound
daily living had inscribed on my hands
and burned it deeper

Empty every pocket at the end of the day
There are other gardens beyond Eden
Bid her leave her clothes folded
on the stones—   beyond the golden acerbic
beyond the idolized violation there moves
a tenderness that shatters and soothes   a river

tell her   its every hand is spread to her

❧ AFTER

Pocket purl rowel gleet: integers of language
chosen for sound alone—scrim lithesome neutrino lute
selvage silvern cistern tithe—   For a long time after the violence

I could collect only single words: caprice careen ganglion hatchet
Later their meanings would flood—inconsolate alluvial slough
huddle fetch lash root—   the way a glass of melting ice plashes

the water from air—chromatic runnel daub ulcerate—   How the surface
festers drops and slakes them down: rend blister titrate cleave—
The way low in the gully after long rains

(grave engrave rubble supine) the re-tethered drops
whispering their trickled diction of return—*seep husk ratchet brute*—
undercut the edge of the paved road

⚘ DAY OF RELEASE

It came first as portent and promise.   Still, I sat years of idle
summers, the percussive dulled and receding.   I forgot
the dream, dismissed love's ruthless
rupture— *(though under the page, below the cement floor,*
ribbons of inexorable muscle beat)

A seepage between stones, it began as trickle, sweet sound,
a small wound, dampness through the house—
Then today!   My chamber of silence split wide.
Released from a prison *(the envelope, the fold)* the underground
shiftings surfaced.   Like an immense flock

the storm waters lifted—*so loud, the run of water—*
and among them were voices I heard as my own.   The sprung
world thundered.   Cracks gave way, and foundations
reared askew.   Concrete was stacked in jagged heaps.
How close and bright the words come!

Among ruins where steam will rise all winter, a river climbs,
labors at its infinite threshold—   *Here I begin!   Reader,*
rip beyond the new-torn banks—   the current exceeds
its wound— *leaving the page   I am leaving—*
jubilant, the sorrowing streams roar.

FLUNG STARS

❧ ❧ ❧ ❧ ❧ ❧ ❧ ❧ ❧

Only when we tarry do we touch the holy.
RAINER MARIA RILKE
Sonnets to Orpheus

❧ HAILSTONE

Twenty-four hours after the storm I pull
another hailstone from the freezer. I seem
to need this cold marble giving itself away,
my wet hand proving a world
of change and I a part of it.

Glacial leakage runs down my wrist—
the sky's art comes *this* close
and dissolves, yesterday turning to old news,
evaporating. I take my light blurred, too:
tiny bulbs gone big and soft

as beach balls diffusing, my father leaping
mid-river to bat the ball. Landing
chest deep, he pressed clear needles
through every plane to catch the last sun.
For so long he was young, then suddenly leaving

himself behind. Pocket lantern of memory,
where can language take me?
The craft is an iceberg, and the days are hot.
Thunderheads burgeon over the ridge,
and every name's become a verb.

Unstoppable, the hail will not be held.
Seeking crevices, now finger, now
thumb, like Helen's first word
slipped under the gush of the pump,
the world flames through our hands.

❦ SOLITUDE AND SAM'S CAT
(above Sonoma, California)

A cat falls in love with me, deeply,
impersonally, as with the sudden thrum of passing
finch wings tonguing the high palate
of sky, though for me Calypso's quick
attention slows. She rubs my writing knuckle,
my jaw with a calico jaw, mammalian bone
to bone. Over the fields of wild oat
and thistle, the columns of breeze are rolling.
This is how I am loved: a noticing desire
follows me in and out of the house, tangles
my ankles, splays on the rug, the bench, stays
near to be near—wanting me and not
for myself—in the manner of June, morning,
this sun, warm wind, the coming poem.

Night Swim
(Northeast Kingdom, Vermont)

I had the need of water round my skin.
Of course it was more: more than faucet rush or fist
of rain, I needed myself kicking my might

against a rolled swiftness where the fall enters
its pool below the rock. I swam alone,
opened my eyes to my own pale skin in a whirling

world going dark. Yellow, pink, ripples
of black, the dusking sky rode uneven gathers
pulled by a body's submerged and quickened thread.

In a river that only moves by shattering itself
and by that process breaks the tyranny of light,
I lay back, and the water held.

I asked, *am I this or am I that?*
When water flowed from the spigot as I washed
my father's hands, we broke silver strands:

the done-unto turned doer, and the holder,
the held. How could we have lived all the years
before, so gladly known by each other,

unknowing the other of ourselves? Our time
is run and the knowledge in our hands exchanged.
He discovered the gifted pleasure of the child

I was (and, tactile, remember), and I
learned the pleasure of bearing the towel. (Did he
in that shifting moment recall it?)

We became more. What once we felt
in part is now nearly whole.
I floated.

My back took to the current, my eyes to the sky.
The night river widened. The pulse of creation
slowed enough for me to perceive it.

LATE SUMMER, MERCED RIVER

The road of excess leads to the palace of wisdom.
WILLIAM BLAKE,
"The Marriage of Heaven and Hell"

The tracks of a Labrador retriever
marked the granite slab where she hauled
her thick body from the body

of the river. Pads of her paws inked
the flecked stone. The dog shook,
and shards of light landed dark.

What love holds itself to its landings?
The arches of summer shimmer. Flung
stars clasp the heat of the day.

They are rising now from the boulders
where all spring the river rode high,
carving its own slick saddle.

❧ The Swimmer

Underwater I became a girl
with a young man's ripe back
the muscles curled
around definite bones

But what you saw from above—
a blue-green daemon fraught with ripple
none of my lines a line—   I was broken
shuffled   yet I moved whole

It is me again   at the far side
surfacing   my face and shoulders
reassembled   solidity of my arms established
the settled years refunded

though where I stand waist-deep in the shallows
my hips   my thighs and feet   approximate
one of Picasso's disarticulated women—
I cannot keep my unshackled forms still

What Auburn Is

The shadowed road closed to all but foot
traffic where the roof of the covered bridge
collapsed under last winter's snow, auburn

is autumn mid-August when among pines
broad leaves of the deciduous lean a brilliant
green toward their yearnings, when after rain

Wendell of the freckles and unloosed, bright hair
walks Zola, the unleashed dog, and from those woods
an unnamed russet pup dances into their path,

and all of them, even the pine needles strewn
thick on the rain-soaked road, lilt so quick
into the late sun beyond the barriers.

❧ TRANSLATIONS
(Sonoma County, California)

The dropped blackberry, picked and reached for
and nearly picked: some things lost are never found.
Seven pairs of reading glasses in just a year
and a half. A contact lens in Lake Tahoe. A retina
tears; I lose parts of my vision.

Waking a second time to the creek's clear
rustle in the dark, the lost is lost and found
again: the needed word; a twelve-year-old
villanelle, "Emily the Cat Had to Comment of Course,"
showed up in a box in my closet.

Some don't matter: I lost my towel and dried off
with my shirt. But once on a deserted tennis court
off Norrbom Road, I endured the footfall of a deer,
suspended. The year before, my lover and I
had spent hours cutting vines.

I carried the clippers and two racquets. She
held the raptor beak of a hedge trimmer. Down
we strode the mile-long hill; our love though
fierce was immortal, then. Within two
solar plexi, the wild elevators

traveled up and down and up through time.
She wore her fine hairs pulled back through the gap
in her turquoise baseball cap. The wind,
when you lie still a long time in the stillness,
begins with a crack and moan of the trees.

A rushing cancels the creek's small clatter
so the larger day of August can open. Then,
the first dry leaves, their premature eagerness
to fly—   Last night late, driving home,
I had to pull off Highway 29—

On the dust of a vineyard lane, I let the engine die.
I fell into Cassiopeia's wide-hipped letter, the last,
and first of the hour, of song, the moment of change.
Because it is simple Greek—that oxymoron—
a translating seminarian begins

with the Prologue to John. When racquetless
and alone I returned, the deer was coming
for the blackberries. Runners were racing again
for the baseline. I sat still on the bench
where we set the ball can, the water bottle,

the jackets we ought not to have brought.
By lob and bounce the deer came down, then stopped,
her right forefoot midair. Our gaze
more steady than any lovers', it seemed hours
until she took her step.   And, another.

Waiting for me not to move and, not moving,
still to speak, a voice only for
the tall, cupped ears—   hoof by hoof
she came, the slowed heartbeat of our forest floor.
She stared so hard, she blinked and blinked again.

There are trees that wait decades for a gale-force
wind, when the leaves roam not aimless
but together. When the cleansing breath
finally roars, those yearning toward autumn
press early from the branch, simply

prologue, while others are torn green.
We were both at once. Some leaves land
soft as the doe turned away—   not fear
but relief, a question resolved.
She bounded—bounded!—up the crashing hill.

Notes

Epigraph page: Henri Bergson, *Creative Evolution*, trans. Arthur Mitchell (New York: Henry Holt, 1911). Adrienne Rich, "Delta," *Time's Power: Poems 1985–1988* (New York: Norton, 1989).

"Elementary Departures": In post-Newtonian physics, atomistic energy events, each inherently relational, constitute the radiant universe. The morning star, a medieval spike-studded ball (as well as a nonindigenous thistle prevalent in Northern California), was twirled overhead to knock enemy riders from their horses.

"Excess" is for Judith Berling and is in debt to Judith Butler and to Jeanette Winterson for the notion that art as "excess" involves the refusal of containment and definition.

"Trick Riders" honors Hazel Walker and Babe Lee, who in 1917 performed as a stunt duo in rodeos along the West Coast from Pendleton to San Francisco, accomplishing their acrobatic maneuvers on a single galloping horse.

"During Migration": The poem draws on Kenn Kaufman's introduction to *Lives of North American Birds* (New York: Houghton Mifflin Harcourt, 2001): "During migration, the rules break down and any birds often show up in unusual habitats. A snipe or a bittern may be found on a city sidewalk, or an ocean-going jaeger may appear on a small inland pond."

"O Yes": In Virginia Woolf's diary entry of 15 September 1924, she writes of Vita Sackville-West: "Oh yes, I like her; could tack her onto my equipage for all time." *The Norton Book of Women's Lives*, ed. Phyllis Rose (New York: W.W. Norton, 1993).

"The Red Boat": The epigraph is from Alfred North Whitehead's *Process and Reality: Corrected Edition* (New York: The Free Press, 1978).

"After Sappho": The epigraph is from Alfred North Whitehead's *Adventures of Ideas* (New York: Free Press, 1933).

"Late Summer, Merced River": The epigraph is from William Blake's "The Marriage of Heaven and Hell," *Selected Poetry and Prose of William Blake*, ed. Northrop Frye (New York: The Modern Library, 1953). "Late Summer, Merced River" is for my brother, the Yosemite fly-fishing guide Tim Hutchins.

"Translations": Cassiopeia's giant "W" is also a small "ω", the last letter of the Greek alphabet. Among the extremely few Greek words that begin with the letter are those that translate to "hour" or "instant" and "ode" or "song of praise." The poem is in conversation with Elizabeth Bishop's "One Art" and is for Alice Templeton.

Acknowledgments

I am grateful to the editors of these publications, in which the following poems first appeared, often in different versions: *Absomaly*: "Day of Release," "Stay / Go"; *Alligator Juniper*: "The Physicist to His Daughter"; *Berkeley Poetry Review*: "O Yes"; *Calyx: Art and Literature by Women*: "The Red Boat"; *Comstock Review*: "Late Summer, Merced River, (as 'September, Merced River')", "Is it"; *Crazy Woman Creek: Women Rewrite the American West* (New York: Houghton Mifflin, 2004): "In a Time of War"; *The Cream City Review*: "The Swimmer"; *88: A Journal of Contemporary American Poetry*: "A Woman's Desperate Hands" (as "Between Here and There"); *Frontiers: A Journal of Women Studies*: "Trick Riders"; *Journal of Feminist Studies in Religion*: "Excess," "The Interstices," "During Migration"; *The Missouri Review*: "Washing My Father's Hands", "Translations"; *Nimrod International Journal*: "Painting Departure," "Hailstone"; *North American Review*: "The Poet to Her Poem"; *Poetry Flash*: "I met a silence"; *Prairie Schooner*: "The Gihon River," "After"; *Roanoke Review*: "Elementary Departures"; *The Southern Review*: "What Auburn Is"; *Spoon River Review*: "Like a tossed rock landed," "Upstream"; *Squaw Valley Review*: "Hail"; *Switchback*: "After Sappho," "Remainders"; *Tampa Review*: "Ripplehalves" (as "Why We Need to Be Together"); *Water-Stone Review*: "Night Swim."

The following poems have been anthologized: "A Poet to Her Poem" (as "A Poem Speaks to the Poet") in *Hello, Goodbye: Stories, Essays and Poems for the 21st Century* (July Literary Press, 2004); "Hailstone" in *The Emily Dickinson Awards Anthology* (Universities West Press, 2005); "The Interstices" and "Trick Riders" in *What I Want from You: Voices of East Bay Lesbian Poets* (Raw Art Press, 2006); "Trick Riders" in *The Great American Poetry Show* (West Hollywood Press, 2004); "Your hands, stained" (as "Black and White Blessing") in *WomanPrayers: Prayers by Women Throughout History and Around the World* (Harper San Francisco, 2003). My gratitude extends to the editors of these anthologies.

"Late Summer, Merced River," "Translations," and "What Auburn Is" appear in the Robin Becker Prize Chapbook *Radiantly We Inhabit the Air*

(Philadelphia: Seven Kitchens Press, 2011). An earlier version of "Your hands, stained" appears in the chapbook *Collecting Light* (Berkeley: Acacia Books, 1999) and was set as a fourteen-minute piece for orchestra and soprano called "Black and White Remembrance" by composer Dan Welcher. It was a finalist for the 2003 Lincoln Center Biennial Prize. "Hailstone" was printed by Littoral Press as a letterpress broadside (2004) for the San Francisco Center for the Book's Poets Pulling Prints, sponsored by *Poets & Writers* and the James Irvine Foundation.

For tangible support, I am glad to thank Money for Women/The Barbara Deming Memorial Fund; Villa Montalvo Center for the Arts (the James Phelan Fund and the Biennial Poetry Prize); Vermont Studio Center; Squaw Valley Community of Writers; *The Missouri Review*'s Jeffrey E. Smith Editors' Prize; and the city of Albany, California.

For crucial encouragement and insight, I am glad to thank David St. John and the members of Sixteen Rivers Press, as well as Robert Hass, Brenda Hillman, Eloise Klein Healy, and my first teacher, the late Thom Gunn. My gratitude also goes to Rebecca Anderson, Judith Berling, Anna Blaedel, Judith Butler, Patricia de Jong, Joseph Driskill, Jane Hirshfield, Sam Keen, Darren Middleton, Marjorie Larney, Melissa Mack, Erica Macs, Ira Sadoff, Catherine Taylor, Alice Templeton, Susan Terris, Peggy Vernieu, and to my cohorts in mischief and mystery, the Cloudview Poets, and the poets of Squaw and Napa. In addition to the late Bruce Hutchins, who continues to live through the love of so many, I thank my beautiful and astute mother, Bessie Hutchins, as well as the other Hutchins and non-Hutchins humans who have extended such patient tenderness to this poet.

PHOTO BY REBECCA ANDERSON

About the Author

CHRISTINA HUTCHINS, Ph.D., teaches philosophy and poetry to graduate students at Pacific School of Religion in Berkeley, California. She holds degrees from University of California , Harvard University, and the Graduate Theological Union and has also worked as a biochemist and as a Congregational (U.C.C.) minister. Her poems have appeared widely in anthologies and periodicals, including *Antioch Review, Beloit Poetry Journal, Denver Quarterly, The Missouri Review, The New Republic, Prairie Schooner,* and *The Southern Review,* and her academic essays have been published in volumes by Ashgate, Columbia University Press, and State University of New York Press. She is the author of two chapbooks, *Collecting Light* (Acacia Books, 1999) and *Radiantly We Inhabit the Air* (Seven Kitchens Press, 2011), which won the Robin Becker Prize. Her literary awards include the *Missouri Review* Editors' Prize, the *National Poetry Review*'s Annie Finch Prize, the James D. Phelan Poetry Prize, and two Barbara Deming Poetry Awards. She lives in Albany, California, where she serves as the city's first poet laureate.

Also from Sixteen Rivers Press:

The Place That Inhabits Us: Poems of the San Francisco Bay Watershed,
  selected by Sixteen Rivers Press
In the Body of Our Lives, by Jeanne Wagner
Inheritance, by Margaret Kaufman
Again, by Lynne Knight
Light, Moving, by Carolyn Miller
Practice, by Dan Bellm
Lucky Break, by Terry Ehret
The Opposite of Clairvoyance, by Gillian Wegener
Today's Special Dish, by Nina Lindsay
In Search of Landscape, by Helen Wickes
The Long Night of Flying, by Sharon Olson
Any Old Wolf, by Murray Silverstein
In the Right Season, by Diane Sher Lutovich
Mapmaker of Absences, by Maria M. Benet
Swimmer Climbing onto Shore, by Gerald Fleming
No Easy Light, by Susan Sibbet
Falling World, by Lynn Lyman Trombetta
Sacred Precinct, by Jacqueline Kudler
What I Stole, by Diane Sher Lutovich
After Cocteau, by Carolyn Miller
Snake at the Wrist, by Margaret Kaufman
Translations from the Human Language, by Terry Ehret
difficult news, by Valerie Berry

Sixteen Rivers Press is a shared-work, nonprofit poetry collective
dedicated to providing an alternative publishing avenue for San
Francisco Bay Area poets. Founded in 1999 by seven writers, the
press is named for the sixteen rivers that flow into the San Francisco Bay.

SAN JOAQUIN • FRESNO • CHOWCHILLA • MERCED • TUOLUMNE •
STANISLAUS • CALAVERAS • BEAR • MOKELUMNE • COSUMNES •
AMERICAN • YUBA • FEATHER • SACRAMENTO • NAPA • PETALUMA